Self-Regulation Skills fo

DEALING with FEELINGS

by Natalia Maguire
Illustrated by Anastasia Zababashkina

ISBN: 978-3-9822799-4-7
Also available as a hardcover book
(ISBN: 978-3-9822799-5-4) and an ebook.

For more information please contact
Natalia Magvayr
Maguire Books
Parkstrasse 8, 22605 Hamburg, Germany

Visit our website at:
www.maguirebooks.com

Illustrator: Anastasia Zababashkina
Instagram @zababashkina_art

Book design: Agata Kananyan
https://www.behance.net/agatakananyan

First printed and bound in the USA.

From the Author

What makes happy and confident adults?

Resilient children—children who believe in their competences, connect to people around them, are secure in their individuality, believe that their actions matter, are able to cope with their emotions and stay in control.

Resilient kids do not collapse because they feel disappointed, frustrated, or angry. They consider negative emotions not as a dead end, but rather an obstacle they can overcome. Or they can turn their negative emotions around to make them work toward their goals.

To some children, this knowledge comes as a gift, but for most of them it is a long learning process, full of mistakes and the usual ups and downs of life. I have written this book to help children get through this process.

I have tried to create engaging short stories about two friends who get into all sorts of real-life situations. They get disappointed, sad, jealous, envious, humiliated, shy, ashamed, scared, offended, and angry. Their wise parents and their desire to stay friends teach them to deal with these seemingly negative emotions and to find positive aspects about them.

Following the short stories are the activity pages to allow kids to look at these feelings from their personal perspective and to develop regulating strategies that work for them.

I hope both you and your children find this book useful and connect even stronger through it.

Contents

Sad Goodbyes

Do you know what Luke dreamt of? Do you think it was a new bike? Or a tablet computer? Or a nice holiday?

Not at all. Luke dreamt that this day would never come. The day when he and his mom and dad would have to move to another city, closer to his grandparents.

Please don't think that Luke didn't love his grandparents. He loved them a lot. But he also loved his friends. Very much so! And he really didn't want to leave them behind. What if he didn't find friends in the new town?

Mom woke Luke up early.
"It's time to get up, Luke. We have a long drive today. We will eat breakfast in the car. Your friends are waiting for you outside. Will you go to say goodbye?"

Dad's car was parked in front of the house. It was so full of luggage it looked like it would explode. Tom and Alex were standing beside it. Teddy was there too.

Teddy was the first to spot Luke. He immediately wagged his tail and ran up to him. Luke stroked Teddy's ear, and Teddy licked Luke's nose.
"Lucky you," Luke thought. "You have no idea what's coming, and don't feel sad."
Tears filled Luke's eyes, but he quickly wiped them away so that his friends wouldn't notice.

"Here, this is for you," Tom said. He handed Luke a gem, which they'd found together on the beach. They almost got into a fight that day, trying to figure out whose gem it was. "You can have it. I'll find another one."
"And this is for you," Alex said as he held out one of the two walkie-talkies on which he and Luke could talk secretly.
"We'll be too far away. The signal will never reach," objected Luke.
"Not necessarily," Alex replied. "See, I attached another antenna to it. We will send a signal through space."
"Sure," confirmed Luke, although he found it hard to believe.

"Luke," Dad called. "It's time to go."
Luke hugged his friends tightly and would not let go, trying to prolong this moment. Tears filled his eyes. Luke hurried to jump into the car so as not to burst into tears in front of his friends.

Dad started the engine, and the car slowly drove away. Luke turned around in the back seat and stared at the figures of his friends for a long, long time. The figures were getting smaller and smaller, and then they disappeared altogether.

And then Luke burst into tears. He cried bitterly, so much so that it was difficult to breathe. He wanted so badly to jump out of the car and run back to where he had been so happy. As if it sensed the moment, a huge black cloud covered the sun, and it stopped shining. Everything was gray. Nothing would be fun or interesting for Luke again.

He felt so sad.

Mom, who was sitting in the back seat too, hugged Luke tightly and said, "I understand that you are sad. I'm sad too. I also had many friends there, a lot of nice memories. But they have not gone anywhere. They are with us—in our hearts. They will always

be with you. And besides, you can still keep in touch with your friends, even when you are far away. True friendship is forever. And I promise that next summer we will visit your friends."

Luke wiped away his tears.

"When you're sad, you need to talk to someone about it," continued Mom. "It helps a lot. Next time, if you feel sad, immediately come to me and say, 'Mom, I'm sad.' You and I will sit down and discuss everything."
"Will that help?" Luke asked somewhat doubtfully.

"Of course it will help. That's the best thing you can do when you are sad. When you talk to someone about your sad feeling, it goes away from you. Now, let's dream of how we will settle down in our new place. Do you know that you will have your own room in our new house? You can decorate it as you wish. What would you like?"

So, Luke talked to his mom about it. Suddenly he realized that he was no longer as sad as he was before. Indeed, he had talked his sadness away.

Luke Gets Inspired

Luke and his parents traveled all day long and only arrived late at night. It was quite dark already. Only Luke did not see that. He had fallen asleep in the car, and Dad had to carry him into their new house.

The next morning Luke woke up because the sun was shining straight into his eyes. It was coming through a large window, which was right opposite the bed.
Luke rubbed his eyes and looked around. He was in a large,

bright room. Only the room was very empty. It only had a bed, a wardrobe, and a table with a chair. And there was nothing else. Nothing at all.
"Hmm," Luke thought. "For the first time, I have my own room. It's so big and so empty."

Dad heard that Luke had woken up and looked into his room.
"Well, have you looked around?" he asked. "What do you think?"
"I like it," Luke answered. "Only there is a lot to be done."
"Of course," Dad replied. "You'll see, your room will be just wonderful. It just needs some work. Come on. I'll show you the rest of the house."

So, Luke went to explore the house. The house turned out to be quite big—much larger than the old one. There were three rooms on the first floor!

Luke ran downstairs and immediately bumped into his grandparents. They had brought delicious pancakes for breakfast.
"Hurrah!" shouted Luke.
"Hurrah!" exclaimed his grandmother and grandfather in reply. "What a big boy you are now!"
Luke tucked a pancake into his mouth and grabbed Grandpa's hand.
"Grandpa, let's go explore!"

It turned out to be quite difficult to move around the house. The ground floor was filled with boxes and furniture, but Luke and his grandfather found a way through them. They checked out the ground floor and then went outside.

"Wow!" Luke called out excitedly when he saw the garden. It was HUGE! Well, okay, not like a park, but almost. There was a big tree near the house, with a real zip line attached. And above it, a treehouse!
"A real treehouse?!" Luke exclaimed and looked at his grandfather. Grandpa winked back at him. "You see, we were really excited to see you, so we got ready!"

Luke climbed up the ladder as quickly as he could and found himself inside the house.
On the inside, the treehouse turned out to be much larger than it seemed from the outside. But it was also empty.

Suddenly Luke came up with a great idea! He knew exactly what he would do! Luke decided to bring to the treehouse everything that reminded him of his old home and his friends. He decided to turn it into his secret place. He could be alone here when he wanted, or he could invite someone if he needed company.

Luke was so excited and had so many ideas. He climbed out of the treehouse and ran into the house.
"Where are the boxes with my things?"

Luke and his grandfather worked all day long. First, they set up things in the treehouse, and then they worked in Luke's bedroom. They didn't even stop to eat. They were so busy.

By evening, Luke's room looked great. Dad had hung shelves on which Luke placed his favorite things. His own drawings were hung on the walls.

Later that evening, when Luke had gone to bed, he suddenly remembered his walkie-talkie.
"Alex, do you read me?" Luke sent a signal into space. But clearly, the signal could not get through.
"Perhaps I need to fix the antenna," Luke thought, slowly drifting off to sleep.

Luke Misses His Friends

The next morning Luke was woken up by rain. The whole sky was overcast. It was wet and cold outside. Luke felt sad and thought about his friends.
"Alex, do you copy?" He tried the radio. No signal came back. Luke took out Tom's gem and squeezed it tightly in his hands.

Mom looked into Luke's room.

"Are you awake? Why aren't you coming down to breakfast?" Then Mom noticed that Luke was upset and sat down on his bed.

"Miss your friends?" she asked.

Luke nodded.

"I understand that you miss your friends. But look at this another way—you have friends who are very dear to you, and you want to be with them. So, you are not alone. It's great when you have people who you love. Time will fly by quickly, and we will soon visit them. Until then, would you like to draw them your treehouse? We can mail your drawing to them. We know the address, right?"

Luke took crayons and paper and ran to his treehouse to draw. Luke drew his new treehouse, and next to it, he drew himself, Tom, Alex, and Teddy. While Luke was drawing, he noticed that his mood got better.

"You see how great it turned out," Mom said when Luke brought her his drawing. "Now, we will mail it to your friends. Imagine how happy they will be to get it. They miss you too. And they are also sad. Now you know what to do when you are sad. When you miss someone, you should talk about this with someone you love. You can tell yourself, 'I will see them soon!' You can look at photos, write letters, draw pictures, and close your eyes and imagine those you miss. You can also call them and talk on the phone."

Mom smiled at Luke and took out a mobile phone from her pocket.

Exciting New Friends

The next morning Luke was sitting in his treehouse. He tried to fix the antenna on the walkie-talkie. Suddenly, he heard voices outside.

Luke looked out and saw a strange sight—a girl was hanging on their fence. She had caught her pants on a nail and couldn't get free. A boy with cool glasses was jumping on the other side of the fence and trying to help. Luke watched carefully, wondering what to do. Suddenly the girl noticed him.
"Come help?" she asked.
Luke quickly climbed down the stairs and ran to the girl.
"Hold me up so that I can get myself free," she ordered.
Luke did not have time to help her. There was a loud ripping sound, and the girl fell directly onto Luke. "Good landing," she said, getting up from the ground and rubbing her forehead.

She had a bump on her forehead and a huge hole in her pants.
"Oh, I'll be in trouble now," she sighed.
"Shall we go to my mom?" Luke proposed. "She can fix it."
"I'm coming with you!" the boy shouted from the other side of the fence. "I'll just walk around."

That day Mom was baking an apple pie. The house smelled so delicious!
Mom was surprised when Luke, the girl, and the boy stood at the doorstep. Mom looked at the kids, and the kids looked at Mom.
"Oh, you've got company. Hungry? Then quickly, get to the table," Mom said.

Mom's pie was a success. The children devoured it, eating quickly without speaking.
"Well." Mom turned to Luke. "Can you introduce your friends?"

Luke was silent. After all, Luke did not know the kids' names.
"I am Lilly," the girl said. "I live next door. And this is Sam." She pointed at the boy with glasses. "He is from another city, and he came to visit us. Can I have more pie, please? It's so tasty." Lilly was now talking non-stop. "You just moved in two days ago, right? I saw a truck with your things." Before anyone could answer, Lilly continued. "It's good that you came. The house was empty for a while. It's boring when there are no neighbors. By the way, what is your name?" she finally asked Luke.
"Luke," he answered.
"Good," Lilly said. "I'm full. Thank you for the pie, but we have to go. We need to explore your garden. Luke, Sam, come." Lilly quickly went to the door.
"Wait, what about your pants?" Luke reminded her.
"Ah ..." Lilly slowed down for a minute and then waved her hand. "It's nothing, I'll fix it at home," she said.

The whole day Luke, Lilly, and Sam played in the garden. Lilly showed Luke the ancient coins that she'd found on the beach near the house. She promised Luke to show him the place another day.

In the evening, Luke could not fall asleep for a long time. Dad came to kiss him good night, and Luke couldn't stop talking about his new friends. He talked and talked, and his heart was beating very loudly. Luke thought it would jump out of his chest. He even got a little scared.
"Dad, my heart is beating so hard," he told him.

Dad laughed.
"You're just overexcited. When you are very excited, it can be difficult to calm down. Do you know how you can help yourself to calm down? You can breathe deeply and drink water. This helps a lot. Let's try to close our eyes and breathe slowly and deeply. I wonder how long it will take us to become completely calm?" So, Luke and Dad began to breathe. One—inhale, two—exhale slowly, three—inhale, four—exhale ...

I wonder which number Luke and his dad counted to?
Luke wouldn't remember, because when he had completely calmed down, he fell asleep.

Bursting With Pride

"Let's go explore our neighborhood," Lilly suggested when she showed up at Luke's house the next morning. "We'll draw a map. After all, you've just arrived, and you don't know that our neighborhood has a lot of interesting and quite unknown places."
"Great idea!" Luke exclaimed.
Of course, he had seen in some films how pirates searched with a treasure map, but Luke himself had never drawn a map. He was very interested.

Luke took out a large sheet of paper and colored pencils. He laid them out on the floor of the treehouse and began to draw a map.
Lilly pointed at the center of the sheet.
"Here are headquarters," she commanded. "And from here, we begin to draw."
"Which headquarters?" Luke asked.
"You are funny," Lilly laughed. "You're sitting in it!"
"Oh, I see!" Luke exclaimed and drew a tree with a small house on it in the center of the sheet.
"And now let's go explore. Let's start with the road to school," Lilly said.
She jumped out of the headquarters and confidently walked away from the house.

Luke and Sam grabbed paper and pencils and ran after her.

There was another large tree to the right of Luke's house, after which the road turned left. The children stopped and drew it on the map.
Then the road went down, and to the left of it, there was a stream. Luke stopped and was about to draw it on the map when he suddenly noticed something flopping in the water.
"Follow me!" he shouted to his friends, and they rushed to the stream.

In the stream, first going under the water and then popping out, a little puppy was fighting for his life. He had somehow fallen into the stream and was now desperately struggling with the current, trying to swim out.

Lilly and Sam froze in surprise and didn't know what to do. But something had to be done. Urgently! Every second counted. Luke knew that one shouldn't go into the water—the stream could be deep, and his mother told him it was dangerous. Luckily Luke noticed a long branch that lay at the edge of the water.

Luke quickly grabbed it and pushed it out into the water. It was long enough to reach the puppy. The puppy held on to it with all his remaining strength, and Luke began to pull the branch with the puppy carefully to the shore.

The poor puppy was so small and wet. And he was trembling—either from the cold or from fear or both. Luke took off his sweater and wrapped the puppy in it.
"We need to take you home where it's warm," Luke told him.
So, the friends hurried to take the puppy to Luke's home and give him some warm milk.

Mom wasn't at home, she had gone to the grocery store. But Dad was at home. He helped Luke pour some milk into a bowl and gave him a towel to wrap the puppy in.
"Tell me what happened?" he asked the kids.
"The puppy was drowning in a stream. And Luke saved him. At the very last moment! Honestly!" Lilly said.
Dad walked over to Luke and shook his hand.
"You're a hero! You saved the puppy's life! Well done!"

"It's true," Luke thought. "I just saved a life!"
Joy filled Luke's heart.
He was very proud of himself.
How wonderful it was to be a hero!

A Bright Side of Disappointment

"Mom! Look who's here!" Luke shouted when Mom came home.
"That's a surprise," Mom said when she saw the puppy. "Where is he from?"
"Your son saved his life," Dad answered proudly. "He pulled him from the stream when the puppy was drowning."
"You went into the stream?" Mom said crossly, looking at Luke.
"No!" Lilly interrupted. "Luke held a large branch, and the puppy grabbed it."
"Such a smart boy," Mom said and kissed Luke. "A real hero!"
"What do we do with you?" Mom asked, looking at the puppy. The puppy, delighted with the attention, did a little wee-wee on the floor, as little dogs do, right in front of Mom.
"Can we keep him?" Luke asked. "Remember Teddy? I miss him. If I could have my own puppy, I would never be lonely."

Mom thought for a moment, and then said, "You know, I don't mind. And Dad, I think, will agree. But we can't just keep the puppy. After all, he may belong to somebody. Imagine if he had just got lost, and somewhere in another house, some child is crying now, thinking he has lost him forever?"
"How can we find out?" Luke asked.
"That's easy. We'll write little notes, and we will post them on the info boards in our neighborhood. If someone is looking for the puppy, they will definitely read it and come to us to collect him. Agreed?"
Luke nodded, even though he was really hoping that no one would come.

Two days passed, and no one had come to collect the puppy. Luke was getting excited. No one might come! Luke started to think of a name for the puppy, until someone knocked on their door.

An elderly woman was standing at the door. She was holding the ad about the puppy. The puppy immediately recognized her. He was so happy! He whined, jumped, and even wee-weed on the floor again. The woman hugged him and cried.

Luke needed no explanation. What was there to explain when everything was clear—that was

the puppy's owner who had come to collect him.
"Thank you," the woman said with tears in her eyes. "I thought I'd never see him again. After all, I have no one except Cookie. I was so lonely. I'm so very grateful to you!"
The woman handed Luke a chocolate bar, put a collar on the puppy, attached a leash, and slowly walked away from Luke's house.

Luke was very disappointed.
He had hoped that no one would come for the puppy, and now his hopes were shattered.

Luke went to his room, sat down in the corner, and curled up in a ball.

Mom and Dad went into Luke's room, sat down next to him, and hugged him.
"I know you're upset," Mom said.
"I saved him ..." Luke cried.
"But you shouldn't be so disappointed. I understand it didn't turn out the way you had hoped. You're sad that the puppy had to go away. But there are two sides to every story. Let's look at it from the other side.
"You have already done one good deed—you saved the puppy. And today we did one more good deed—we helped an elderly woman who was feeling very lonely. After all, if you hadn't saved the puppy and we hadn't started looking for the owner, she would have been so sad."

Luke thought about it. Yes, he was sad. But the woman who found her puppy was so happy. And it was he, Luke, who had made that happen.

Mom said, "It is wrong to hide it when you get upset. It is better to discuss it with someone you trust. Disappointment is similar to sadness. When you talk to someone, it always gets easier. Now, do you feel better?"
"I do," Luke said with surprise.

Now Luke knows that every situation has two sides. And in any disappointment, one can find something positive. One only needs to look for it.

Luke got up and ran to Lilly. Perhaps, there were more good deeds to be done.

A Lesson in Shame

"Today is my mom's birthday," Luke said proudly to Lilly as they walked by the stream. "She said you could come to our house to celebrate and have dinner with us."
"That's great," Lilly answered. "Do you have a present for her?"
"No," Luke replied. "But I learned a poem about moms, and I will tell it to the guests who come today."
"That's great. I don't know any poems about moms. And I don't have a gift. What should I do?" Lilly said thoughtfully.
"I have an idea!" she exclaimed. "Let's collect a bunch of wildflowers for your mom!"
So, Luke and Lilly went to look for flowers.

Sadly, they were not very lucky. Only grass and bushes were growing near the stream. Luke and Lilly found only two small flowers, and even they were not very pretty.
"This isn't enough for a bouquet," Lilly said.
"Yes," Luke agreed. "Mom doesn't have such a small vase."

Luke and Lilly were on their way back home when suddenly they saw a huge patch of daisies near one of the houses. They were so beautiful, and they smelled great!
"Let's pick those daisies? Look how beautiful they are!" Lilly suggested.
"Can we?" Luke sounded unsure. "These are garden flowers. People probably planted them on purpose. We should ask for permission."

"No," argued Lilly. "What if they won't allow it? Where will we get the flowers then? There are so many flowers here, no one will notice."

So, Luke and Lilly picked some daisies. What a beautiful bouquet they had!

"Mom, come here!" Luke shouted from the doorway. "We have a gift for you!"
"What a beautiful bouquet!" Mom said. "Thank you so much!"
Mom put the bouquet in a vase and put it on the table. It was clear that she really liked the flowers.

But suddenly, they heard the doorbell.
Mom opened the door. An unfamiliar woman stood on the threshold.
Luke and Lilly didn't hear what she said to Mom. But Mom called them to come to the door.
"Luke, Lilly, tell me, where did you get these flowers?" asked Mom.

Luke and Lilly looked at each other, not knowing what to say.
"We picked them on the way home," Lilly finally said.
"But where exactly?" asked Mom.
Luke and Lilly stared at the floor. They did not dare to raise their heads.
"That's not good!" Mom said. "You stole flowers and brought them to me as a gift? That's not such a good gift." Mom was sad. She said something to the stranger and closed the door behind her.

Luke and Lilly stood by the door and did not move.
They were ashamed!
Their cheeks turned red, and they began to cry.
"Do you feel ashamed?" Mom asked.
"Ye-e-e-e-s," the children said, sobbing.
"Well, it's good that you feel ashamed. It means you have a conscience. Let's wipe away your tears and think about what we should do."

Mom gave each child a glass of water and sat them on the sofa in front of her. Mom spoke.
"You did something not very nice today. Even two things. First, you stole the flowers. Even though it was to make me happy, you should never take other people's things without asking. Second, you tried to lie about where you got them. Tell me, if no one would have noticed you, would you not have felt guilty?"

The kids didn't say a word. They were ashamed to look at Mom.
"I know you would have felt guilty," Mom continued, "because you are good and kind children. You made a mistake. What should happen with mistakes?" Mom asked and answered herself. "We should always learn from them and correct them. Now think about how you can correct your mistake."
"We'll go apologize," Luke said.
"And we will work in the garden to make it even more beautiful," Lilly suggested.
"I think that's a good idea," Mom responded. "You know where to go, right?"

Luke and Lilly went to the garden where they had picked the flowers. They stood in front of the door for a long time and did not dare to ring the doorbell. But suddenly, the door opened. They saw the woman who came to their mother.

"We came to apologize," Luke said.
"We are very sorry," Lilly continued. "And we would like to do

something for you to correct our mistake."
"We are ashamed of ourselves," Luke confirmed.
"Well," the woman said, "everyone makes mistakes. The most important thing is to understand your mistake and, if you can, fix it in time. I have jobs for you. You, Lilly, need to water the flowers in the front garden with a big watering can, and you, Luke, can collect the dry leaves from the lawn."

Luke and Lilly worked so hard! They made sure that not a single leaf or twig remained on the lawn and that all the flowers were very well watered.

When the work was finished, they rang the doorbell.
"We've finished," Luke said. "Please check if everything is fine."
The woman went out to look.
"Wow!" she exclaimed. "Great work! Thank you! For that, you deserve a little something."
Luke and Lilly were surprised.
"Come with me," she said, and led them to the rose beds. "You can each choose one flower, and I will cut them for you."
"This one, please." Lilly pointed to the yellow rose.
"And for me, this one, please." Luke pointed to the red rose.

The woman cut the roses and handed them to the children.
"Carry them carefully," she said. "Watch out for the thorns."
"Thank you," Luke said. "Will you forgive us?"
"Yes, of course," the woman answered. "Just don't do that again, okay?"
Luke and Lilly happily nodded and ran as fast as they could to Luke's house.

That day Luke and Lilly learned that when they feel ashamed, it is because they have done something bad. So they need first to understand what they did wrong and then apologize and correct the mistake. And everything will be fine again!

Facing Fear in a Thunderstorm

"Dad and I are going camping this weekend," Luke said to his mom with excitement as he ran into the house. "He found a tent in the garage!"

"Not the best idea," Mom said. "Look at the weather forecast. There will be a storm."

Luke was upset to hear that as he really wanted to go camping.

Dad stroked his head.

"Don't worry," Dad said. "Maybe the thunderstorm will miss us. We won't go far. We'll put up a tent in the garden."

"Right in our garden?" Luke was surprised. "Can we do that?"

"Of course!" Dad smiled. "Then your mom won't be worried."

Mom smiled.

"I'll prepare some food and a flask of tea," she promised. "We don't want you starving, do we?"

On Saturday afternoon, Dad took the tent out of the garage and brought it into the garden. Luke helped Dad carry sleeping bags, pillows, matches, and the food that Mom had prepared for them.

Suddenly, Lilly appeared.

"What are you doing?" she asked.

"We're going camping!" Luke answered proudly. "In a real tent, and we are sleeping here overnight!"

"Can I join you?" Lilly continued hesitantly.

"Of course," Luke's dad replied. "There's room enough for everyone. But you need to ask your mom first."

"I'll be quick," shouted Lilly, already running to ask her mom.

A little later, Lilly returned.

"Mom said I can," she said, smiling.

She had changed into comfortable, clean clothes and had brought a pillow and blanket with her.

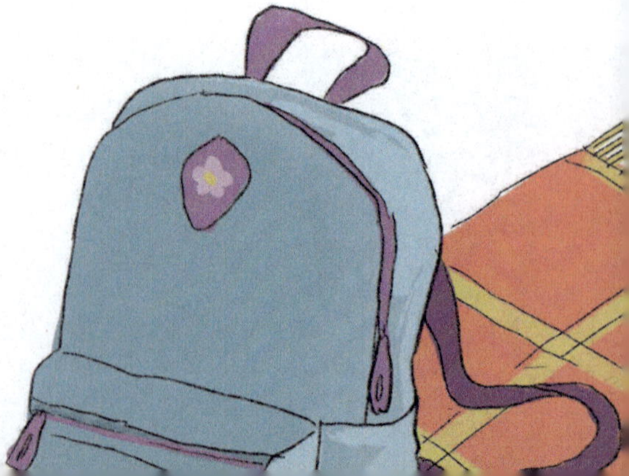

Luke, Lilly, and Dad gathered all they needed in one spot. Even though they were in their garden, it felt somehow as if they were far from home.
"Now the adventure begins!" Luke thought happily.

And he was right.
To begin with, Luke and Lilly had to put up the tent. Dad explained to the kids what to do, and they did it very well.
"Next time, you can do it without my help!" Dad said encouragingly when they had finished.

Then, it was time to light a fire. This was very exciting for Luke and Lilly as they were not allowed to play with matches. Dad told them exactly what to do and how to do it safely, and in no time, they had a lovely warm campfire.
"Well done!" Dad said.

Luke and Lilly were thrilled that their first camping trip was going so well. Finally, Dad took out the food, and the kids started to grill sausages over the fire. The sausages turned out to be smokier but tastier than usual.
"I could eat these sausages every day!" Luke said.
"Yeah," Lilly agreed. "Delicious!"

It was getting dark. Sparks from the fire rose into the sky like fireflies. They slowly flew upward and then disappeared into the dark sky. The children and Dad sat near the tent eating their sausages. Everything was great until ...
... the thunder crashed. It sounded like an angry, growling animal.

Luke and Lilly jumped up and looked at the sky—a huge cloud hung over the tent. Lightning flashed. The children clung to Luke's dad.
"Are you scared?" Dad asked.
"It's growling!" Luke said.
Dad smiled.
"Now think: who can growl at you from the sky? Thunder is just a sound, and it is not dangerous at all!"
"And the lightning?" Luke asked.

"Now that's different," Luke's dad replied, and he began to explain. "Lightning is electricity, the same that makes the bulbs go on in our house. But lightning is much stronger. When there is too much of it in the clouds, the clouds need to get rid of it. So they throw it down to earth. When that happens, we hear thunder."

"If lightning is electricity, then isn't it dangerous?" asked Luke.

"Not when it's far away," Dad replied, to Luke's surprise. "Look, when we have electricity at home, we are not afraid of it. As long as we do not touch it, everything is safe, right?"

"Of course!" Luke agreed. He knew that for sure!

"Same here; when there is lightning, the most important thing is not to let it touch you. For that, one needs to hide in a house or under a bridge, for example. If you hide correctly, then the lightning will never harm you!"

While Luke's dad was telling them all this, lightning flashed in the sky again. Then Dad began to count:
"One, two, three ..."
"What are you counting?" Lilly asked him.
"I am trying to understand how far away the thunderstorm is. During a thunderstorm, we see light and hear sound. They both start at the same time and in the same place. But light travels very fast. Faster than any rocket! Just because we see lightning, that doesn't mean at all that it is nearby. Sound travels more slowly. I am counting the time it takes to reach us. This is how I can figure out how far away the lightning is. Do you want to try to count with me?"

Luke and Lilly nodded. When they saw the next bolt of lightning, they began to count.
"One, two, three, four, five ..." and they counted to ten.
It was only then that they heard the thunder.
"You see," Dad said, "since we could count to ten, then the storm is still far away! But when you only manage to count to five, it's time to hide!"

Luke was relieved to hear that they weren't in any danger. "Dad, could the storm not come any nearer?"
"Of course," Dad replied. "Let's keep counting. Then we will understand whether we need to hide or not."

Luke and Lilly each took the last sausages and began to look at the sky. When the lightning flashed again, they began to count: "One, two, three, four, five, six, seven ..." Thunder.
"Oh! It's getting closer," Dad said.

Another bolt of lightning and Dad started counting. This time he only reached five.
"It's time to find shelter!" Dad exclaimed, quickly putting out the fire and taking the pillows under his arm. Luke wanted to shelter in the tent, but Dad rushed them all back into the house.

As Luke and Lilly ran to the house, they felt the first drops of rain.

Mom had already opened the door and was waiting for them.
"Well, how was your camping trip?"
"Great!" Luke said enthusiastically.
"Only I was a bit scared of the thunderstorm," Lilly said. Luke and Dad realized that they hadn't noticed how scared Lilly had been.
"My heart was pounding," said Lilly, "and I could feel myself shaking."
"Are your hands sweating? Did you feel like hiding? Did you want someone to give you a big hug?"
"Yes," Lilly said. "How did you know?"

Mom hugged Lilly tightly and said, "I know how fear feels. I am also sometimes afraid. But fear isn't a bad feeling. Sometimes fear protects you and warns you that danger is near. For example, I am afraid of wasps and bees because they can sting me. I am afraid of fire because it can burn. But when I am afraid, I know how to deal with it."
"But how?" Luke and Lilly asked.

"There are many ways." Mom answered.
"First, it is better to tell your mom or dad or a friend that you are afraid. When you share your fears, others can show you that

there is nothing to be afraid of. Second, try to think of how you can protect yourself. For example, now you are in the house where lightning cannot get you. So, you are safe and there is nothing to be afraid of. And third, you can draw your fear. It helps you get it out of your mind."
"I know a better way," Dad interfered. "Draw your fear in a funny way. After that, whatever you are afraid of will not be so scary."
"Let's draw a funny thunderstorm. Who can suggest how?" Luke's mom asked while putting paper and colored pencils on the table.

Feeling offended

"Luke, have you seen what's happening?" Lilly shouted as she stood by the front door. "Remember the old house at the end of our street? It is being ripped down! A big machine is taking it apart with its huge claws! It's so cool! Come, see!"
Luke quickly pulled on his boots and ran after Lilly.

And there it was. A huge machine was knocking the house down, lifting each piece and loading it into a truck. It was really noisy and dusty.
"Wow!" Luke said in amazement. He had never seen anything like this before.
Luke and Lilly stood and watched.
Only, not for long. The house disappeared very quickly. When the trucks left, instead of a house, there was only a big hole.

Luke and Lilly wanted to explore it and moved closer. Suddenly Luke noticed something shiny on the ground near Lilly.
"What is that, Lilly?" Luke asked and pointed at it.
"Oh," Lilly said, excitedly. "It's a coin! A real coin! Hurrah! I found a coin!"

Lilly gripped the coin tightly in her hand and jumped for joy.
Luke couldn't believe it.
"You found it?" Luke said in surprise.
"I found it. I found it!" Lilly sang as she danced in a circle.
"But I spotted it first, so the coin is mine," Luke objected. "Or, it belongs to both of us. Shall we share it?" he suggested to Lilly.
"Well, it's a coin, so we cannot cut it in two. I picked it up first. So, it's mine!" Lilly insisted.
"But that's not fair! We are friends!" Luke exclaimed.
Lilly didn't answer. She gripped the coin tightly in her hand, turned around, and quickly ran home.

Luke was so annoyed and hurt by Lilly's behavior. He couldn't believe she had really done that. Feeling very sad, Luke returned home and told Mom what had happened.

"That was so unfair," Luke said.
"I understand," Mom said. "I agree with you. What Lilly did was not right. And you have the right to feel offended. Only it is a very unpleasant feeling. Feeling offended is like ropes that bind you and prevent you from moving on and enjoying life. When you are offended, you can stay in a terrible mood for a very long time. Sometimes, it can last for weeks and even months."
"What should I do?" Luke asked. "How do I make myself feel good again?"
"Look, if you sit at home and sulk, the hurt will definitely not go away. You need to talk to Lilly. Wait for Lilly to come to you and talk to her."
"And what should I tell her?"
"You can say: 'What you did, Lilly, was wrong. Friends do not behave like that. I was hurt by what you did.'
"Also, it is good to suggest what would make it right. For instance:
'You could buy something with the coin that we both can share.'"

"Good," Luke agreed and sat down to wait for Lilly to come to him.
But Lilly didn't come.
Luke was very bored sitting alone. So, he decided that he would make the first move and go to Lilly to talk to her.

Luke put on his shoes, threw open the door, and, to his surprise, he saw Lilly, who was standing at the door.

"I was really hurt by what you did," Luke said calmly, and he immediately noticed how he felt better. "It was not fair."
Lilly replied,
"I am sorry, Luke. I know what I did was wrong. We found this coin together. Let's spend it together? Let's go to the kiosk and buy some ice cream?"
"Sure!" Luke exclaimed happily.

So, Luke and Lilly bought themselves ice cream. Luke got a scoop of chocolate ice cream, and Lilly got vanilla, her favorite. The ice cream was delicious.

As Luke ate his ice cream, he thought,
"The coin was, of course, valuable. But my friendship with Lilly is much more valuable. It's great that we are friends again!"

One Step at a Time

"Look what I brought!" Lilly screamed as soon as she came in the door.
Luke peered more closely.
Lilly was holding two large packs of paper cups. About 100 cups, if not more ...
"Why do you need so many?" Luke asked, surprised.
"Not why do I need so many. But why do we need so many!" Lilly replied. "We are going to build a skyscraper with them! Look!"

Lilly handed Luke a picture of a large tower built from paper cups.
Luke had seen such a tower before. His cousin Paul built it once, and it looked really easy to do.
"What is there to learn?" Luke exclaimed confidently. "It's as easy as pie."
He took the cups from Lilly's hands, unwrapped them, laid the cups out on the carpet, and started to build.

Luke was sure that he could do it easily, but he was in for a surprise—no sooner had he placed the first cups down than his tower collapsed. He didn't even get a chance to build the lowest floors.
Luke started again—another disaster.
Once again, the tower collapsed. But why?

Luke was getting angry. He started to breathe faster and louder. His hands clenched into fists, and he seemed to be trembling inside.
"There's something wrong with these cups. I won't build with them!" Luke said angrily, kicking the cups. Cups flew all over the room.

At that moment, Luke's dad entered the room. "Wow! What did the poor cups do to you?"
Luke stared at the carpet, not saying a word.
"We are trying to build a tower from paper cups, like this one." Lilly showed Luke's dad the picture. "Luke said it was simple. But we can't."
"How did you build it?" Dad asked. "Show me!"

Luke started building again, and the tower fell apart again. Luke was very upset.
"I see that you are frustrated," Dad said. "You are trying to do everything too quickly and not step by step. That's the wrong approach."
"How should we do it then?" Lilly asked. Luke was also interested to hear.

"Imagine you want to run a marathon. It is slightly longer than 26 miles. You have to run for many hours without stopping. Do you think you can do it?" Dad asked.
Luke and Lilly shook their heads.
"Of course not," Dad agreed. "And I can't do it either. And even our Uncle Sam, who is very fit, wouldn't be able to do it. But that never means that you have to give up and not even try. If you really want something, then you must definitely try to do it. But don't rush into it."

"Should we wait?" Lilly asked.
"Not quite," Dad said. "You just need to break everything into small steps and do one step at a time. For example, take a marathon—those who want to run a marathon start off slowly. They run, say, only one or two miles at first, then five miles, then ten miles. And so, gradually, they learn to run long distances. They learn to move and breathe correctly. Muscles become stronger, and their stamina increases. So, only after regular training can a person finally run a marathon.

"But you and I, fortunately, have a simpler task. We don't need to train for so long. I promise you, by the end of today, you will have built a huge cup-tower."

Luke and Lilly's eyes lit up.

FINISH
START
2 miles
5 miles
10 miles

"The first step is the most important," Dad said. "We need a positive attitude. We must believe that we will definitely succeed if we do not rush and if we try our hardest.

"For example, if I say to myself, 'This is not as difficult as it seems,' what will you say to yourselves? No copying now!" Dad smiled.

"We can do this!" shouted Luke.

"I believe in us!" exclaimed Lilly.

Lilly and Luke's moods improved immediately.

"Step two—analyze the task," Luke's dad continued. "You need to take a close look at the problem and analyze what is important. Let's take a look at the picture Lilly brought. What is the tower standing on?"

"On the table," Luke answered.

"And what did you build on?" Dad asked.

"The rug," said the children, and they looked at it closely.

"Do you see the difference?" asked Dad.
"It's uneven!" exclaimed Lilly. "That's why the tower fell!"
"Exactly," Dad agreed. "Let's build on the floor. It's as flat as a table."

So, the kids moved from the rug to the wooden floor.
"Now try building." Luke's dad said. "And make sure that each floor is perfectly straight before you build the next one."

Luke and Lilly started building. And they succeeded!
The tower turned out to be very high. A real skyscraper!
"Hooray! We did it!" the children cheered.
"And it wasn't difficult at all!" Luke smiled slyly.

Luke Sails His Worry Away

"Granny is very sick," Mom said to Luke one evening. "She has been taken to the hospital. Your dad and I need to go there to be with her. You're going to spend the night at Lilly's, okay?"

Luke sensed something was really wrong.
Mom looked very worried, although she tried not to show it. Luke knew that something very serious had happened to his grandmother.
"I will see her again, won't I?" Luke asked nervously. He really loved his grandmother.
"Of course you will. The doctors will take good care of her. It's just very important now that your dad and I are with her," Mom replied.
Luke nodded. Mom packed his things and quickly took him to Lilly's house.

All evening Luke could not relax. He was very worried about his grandmother and was afraid that he would not see her again. Lilly and her mother tried to entertain Luke and distract him from his upsetting thoughts, but nothing worked.

Soon it was time to go to bed. Lilly fell asleep quickly, but Luke still could not calm down. All he could think about was his grandmother and when he would see her again. As soon as he closed his eyes, he always imagined the worst outcomes, and he just couldn't stop himself.

The next morning was no better—Luke had a stomach ache, and his head was still full of worries about his grandmother.
"That's not going to do any good," Lilly's mom said. "Why are you letting your worries get bigger and bigger?"
"I can't control it. They grow on their own," Luke answered sadly.
"That's not true," Lilly's mother said. "When you think about your worries, you make them grow. It's like with a flower, or with a tree—you water it, and it grows more and more."
"What can I do?" Luke asked.

"I know what you can do! Just wait!" Lilly exclaimed and ran to her room. After a few seconds, she came running back, holding a box. She plopped the box down on the table and opened it. "Look!"
At the bottom of the box, there were several small, handmade dolls.

"Meet George," Lilly proudly announced. "This is my fear of getting lost. Once, when my mom and I were in a huge shopping center, I got lost and was very scared. And now, I sometimes worry about getting lost again, and it makes me sad. When I want to think about it, I take George out and think about that day. Then I put him back in the box so that my worry goes away."
"Why did you call him George?" Luke asked.
"I don't know," Lilly said. "It just came to me."

"And this one ..." Lilly took out a bright orange doll from the box. "This is Lightning. Remember when we went camping, and I got scared in the thunderstorm? So, I made this doll, and with it, I am not afraid when there is a thunderstorm."

"This is Chris. He ..." Lilly paused. "I won't tell you. Guess!"
Luke looked at Chris. The doll was black and shaggy.
"He looks like a spider," Luke said.
"Hooray! You guessed it!" Lilly cried.
"One day, a spider crept into my room. He climbed right onto my pillow. Ugh! It was disgusting. Since then, I am worried that a spider will come into my room. So, I made Chris. When I start thinking about spiders, I immediately get him out of the box to help me with my worry.

He always helps! Let's make a doll about your worry over your grandmother, and then we'll make your worry go away."

"Great idea!" Mom said, and she fetched wooden ice cream sticks, felt-tip pens, and a lot of colorful yarn and put them all on the table.

Luke tried very hard. He wanted the doll to turn out right and to help him with his worries.

He decided to make it blue, like a doctor's uniform. And he painted the face so that it was beautiful and kind like his grandmother. While he was making the doll, he thought about his grandmother and how he wanted her to get well as soon as possible.

"I've finished," Luke said proudly, and he looked closely at his doll. It doesn't look very much like my grandmother. More like the doctor who is treating her, Luke thought.

Suddenly Luke realized something. While he was making the doll, his worries disappeared.
"That's a cool doll." Lilly interrupted Luke's thoughts. "Are you still worried?"
"Not at all," Luke said, surprised.
"Told you! It always works for me too. But we're not done yet. Now you need to make a house for your worry doll. It is

important to hide it there and to take it out only when it can help you. Here, I have an extra box, and the size fits perfectly. Let's make a house together for your worry doll."

That day, Luke didn't worry nearly as much as previously. And when he began to worry, he immediately took out the doll from the house and talked to her. And she always calmed him down!

And then finally Luke's mom called! His grandmother was doing well! And best of all, Luke would be able to visit her soon!

"Well," Lilly said. "You don't need this doll anymore. Let's build a boat and send your doll on a long journey along the stream and let your worries go away for good!"
"No," objected Luke. "Not so quick. I still need it. But when my granny returns home, then we'll sail my worry doll away!"
So Luke and Lilly went to build a boat.

Standing Up to Bullies

Grandpa bought Luke a football! How beautiful it was! Luke was so happy!

"Look, Lilly! This is a real football, not a kid's one! Real players on TV play with this. When I grow up, I will be a famous football player!"

"But are you good enough?" Lilly was doubtful.

"Of course I am. Now I have the right ball. All I need to do is practice. Let's go to the football pitch near the school. You can help with my training," Luke suggested.

So off they went.

The field was wet after the rain, but Luke and Lilly found a dry spot near the goal.
"Stand there," Luke instructed. "I'll shoot, and you can be the goalkeeper."
"Okay," Lilly said.

But not a single goal was scored. Not because Lilly was a great goalkeeper, but because Luke couldn't kick the ball on target.
"Missed again," Lilly said. "Come closer."
"I'm just warming up. I need to get used to this ball." Luke was still confident.

Suddenly some boys came onto the field. They were older than Luke and Lilly. By chance, Luke's new ball rolled up to one of them and hit him on the leg. The boy stopped the ball and put his foot on it.
"Sorry," Luke said politely. "I didn't mean it. Can I have the ball back?"
But the bigger boy didn't want to give it back.
"We need to think," he said slowly and grinned. "I don't like the way you are asking." His friends laughed. It was clear that these were not kind boys, and one could expect nothing good from them.

"But that is Luke's ball," Lilly cried. "Give it back, please!"
"And who is this squeaking?" The boys burst out laughing. "A mosquito?"

They began to throw the ball between themselves.
Poor Luke and Lilly ran after the ball, but they could not catch it. The bad boys thought this was very funny. They laughed loudly and teased poor Luke and Lilly.
"Well, why are you running so slowly? Come on. You almost got it! You need to run quicker!" they said in a mocking tone.
Luke and Lilly were exhausted.

Finally, the older boys got tired of playing.
"Okay," one of them said. "We will give you the ball. Only you must first ask us for it. On your knees!"

What should he do?
Luke felt completely defenseless. It seemed to him that he was decreasing in size—becoming smaller and smaller. His head sunk into his shoulders. All he really wanted was to run away from these boys, but he had to get his ball back. Luke was about to kneel when Lilly stopped him.

"You have no right! You have no right to do this to us!" she shouted. "Give us the ball back!"

Lilly stood straight, confidently lifting her head. This made her seem taller and even a little older. She looked very sure of herself and powerful, despite being small.
"What?" The boy wasn't expecting that.
"Give the ball back!" Lilly repeated. "Or we will call our parents!"

"Here, take it then," the boy said.
Then he took a nail out of his pocket and burst the ball in front of everyone. The air whistled out of the ball as it flew into a puddle next to Luke and Lilly. When it landed, it was no longer a ball, just a flat piece of colored leather.
Luke and Lilly picked it up and quickly ran home.

On the way, they met Luke's dad. He was driving home from work and saw Luke and Lilly, who looked really upset. Dad knew right away that something was wrong.
"They ruined my ball!" Luke said, sobbing. "This was all Lilly's fault. I should have asked on my knees!" Luke looked angrily at Lilly.
Dad's eyebrows went up high on his forehead.
"Where are they?" Dad asked angrily and hurried to the soccer field.
The field was empty. In the distance, he could see some boys running away.

Dad sat down on the ground next to Luke and Lilly and listened carefully to what had happened. And then Dad said, "The boys were wrong. What they did was bad. I know they seemed big and strong to you. They were not strong. **A strong person would never humiliate a person who is clearly weaker. In fact, a strong person would never humiliate anyone at all. Only a weak person who does not believe in his own strength can offend someone weaker.**

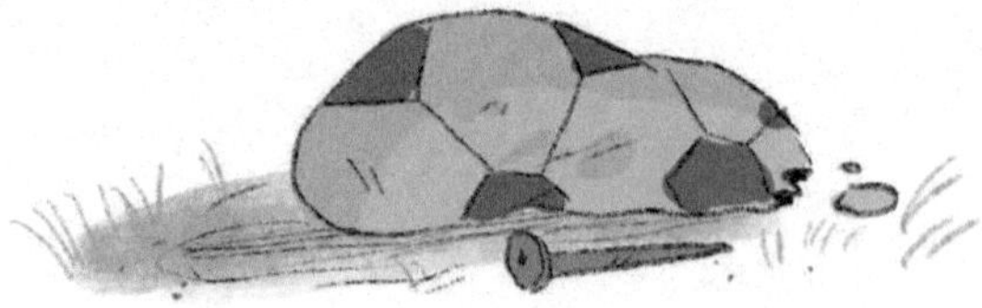

"Remember, no one ever has the right to humiliate or offend you. Nobody ever!
You cannot allow yourself to be humiliated!"

"But what could we do?" Luke wondered.
"Exactly what Lilly did," Dad replied. "She did the right thing! If someone wants to humiliate you, you need to show them that you are confident. Stand up straight, hold your head up, and say,
'I don't like that! You can't do that to me. Stop it!'
Walk away.
Don't let them tell you hurtful things!
As soon as they see that you do not care and are not afraid of them, they will stop.
And if you feel like you need help, come to Mom or me."

Luke thought about it.
"You're right," he sighed. "Lilly did the right thing."
Now he knows how not to let himself be humiliated.
And someday, he too will be able to defend others!

A Touch of Envy

"Who draws like that?" Lilly asked Luke, looking at his drawing. "I don't get it! Your crocodile looks like"—and Lilly paused, thinking—"like a rat!"
"It's you who looks like a rat!" Luke shouted. "A nasty rat that believes that she is the best but can't even ride a bike properly!"
"I can't ride a bike? I can ride much faster than you can!"
"And anyway, you ... you are just a girl, a squeaking girl who thinks that she knows everything better than anyone else!" Luke exploded.

Lilly could not bear it any longer.
Her lower lip quivered, her shoulders shook, tears welled up in her eyes, and she ran out of Luke's house.

"What's got into you?" Mom asked in surprise, having heard all the fuss. "I've never seen you like this."
"Nothing!" Luke blurted out angrily.

He sat down on the sofa, hugged his knees, and stared angrily somewhere.

Mom came over and sat down next to him.
"But you can't have offended Lilly for no reason at all." Mom said.
"There was a reason!" Luke answered grimly. "I'm sick and tired of her!"
"Why are you sick and tired of her?" Mom could not understand.
"I'm sick of everything! She always knows how to do everything better—she can ride a bicycle without hands, she reads better than I can, she draws better. And also," Luke hesitated a little, "she has just been invited to a birthday party. In the best trampoline park! And I have never been there."

"Now I see," Mom said. "The situation is somewhat dangerous."
"Dangerous?" Luke was surprised.
"Dangerous," Mom said again. "It is dangerous because you envy Lilly and do not know what to do about it. And envy is an awful feeling."
"Why is it bad?" Luke asked.
"Envy is like a worm that grows inside you. At first, it is small and hardly noticeable. But then it grows and grows until one day, like today, it begins to control you and push you to do bad things. Envy hurts both the people who are jealous and the people they are envious of. Friendships break down, and people feel so unhappy. So unhappy, in fact, that if you are envious for a long time, it can make you sick."
"I don't want to get sick," Luke said.

"And you won't," Mom assured, "because I'll teach you how to get rid of it. Look, you envy Lilly because she can do something better than you, or she has something that you don't, right? That is, you are looking at her. But you have to look at yourself and think of what is good in you."
"There's nothing I'm better at." Luke seemed frustrated. "She does everything better."
"That can't be true. Every person has something that makes them better. Just think about it," Mom suggested.

Luke thought about it.

"I ... I can fold paper airplanes that fly very far!" Luke exclaimed happily.
"What else?"
"And also ... I can make a delicious pizza. And I have the most interesting dreams! And I can solve difficult puzzles and build really hard construction sets. And I know how to hide well so that no one can find me. And I can read poetry well, and I can sing! And, I can also move my ears! Look!"

Luke's eyes sparkled. He was very pleased with himself.

"You see how wonderful and special you are!" Mom smiled.
"This is how, in everyone, absolutely in every person, you can find the most wonderful and interesting qualities and talents. And if everyone were the same, then we would not have the best athletes, cooks, doctors, scientists, teachers, and ..."
"... and moms!" Luke said, and hugged Mom tightly.
Mom smiled and replied.
"I think that you need to remember another talent of yours—a talent to be a good friend. What do you think?"

Luke didn't reply. He turned and quickly ran to the door.

Saying Sorry

Knock-knock. Luke knocked on the door of Lilly's house. Knock-knock.
Lilly's mom opened the door. She looked at Luke seriously and said, "I think now is not the best time. Please come back later."
"I can't wait," Luke objected. "I am sorry for what I've done, and I came to apologize."
"Well, in that case ..." Lilly's mom said, and let him into the house.

Lilly was sitting on the floor in the middle of the carpet. Her face was all red and wet with tears. Her back rose and fell again, without stopping, because she was crying so much. She heard Luke's voice and quickly turned away from him. She didn't want to see him.

"I came to apologize," Luke said. "I am so sorry for shouting at you and saying all those bad things. I didn't think about what I was saying. I was very envious. I was just upset that you can do so many things better than I can—you can ride a bike, draw, and do so many more things better than I can. You are really talented and brave!"

Lilly's back stopped twitching. She calmed down as she listened very carefully to Luke.
Luke continued: "To be honest, you're so good at things, well, I was envious. And a huge nasty worm grew in me!"
Lilly turned and looked at Luke. She was shocked.
"A huge worm?" Lilly's eyes opened wide.
"An envy worm that grew and grew until I told you a bunch of bad things. I am very sorry. Can you forgive me?"

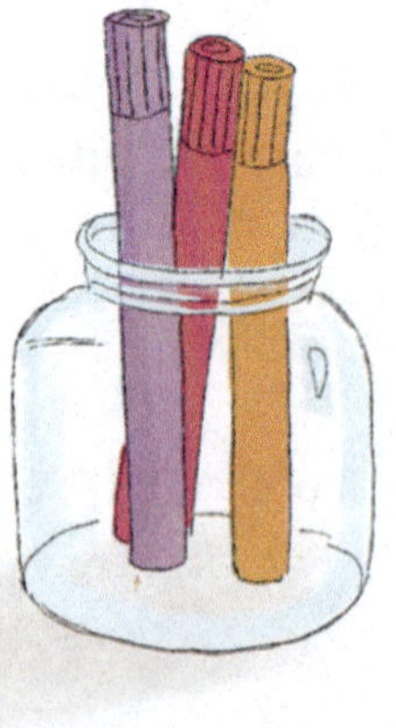

"And this worm, does it still live in you?" Lilly asked, not liking the thought of a worm living in Luke.
"Not anymore," Luke said confidently. "I beat him."
"But how?" Lilly still found it all hard to understand.
"I realized that everyone has talents, both you and me and everyone else. Each person has different talents, and that's great. You shouldn't feel envious, but you should be happy about your talented friends and their successes. And then the envy worm won't live inside you."

"You're so smart!" Lilly said suddenly. "Do you want me to teach you how to draw well? It's not difficult at all."
"Really?" Luke exclaimed happily. "Does that mean you've forgiven me?"
"Of course!" Lilly answered. "Because I have another talent—I can forgive!"

Lilly took Luke by the hand, and together they ran to Luke's house—to learn how to draw a crocodile.

Sibling Rivalry

Dad lifted Luke and threw him up high!
"Congratulations!" Dad said happily to Luke. "You are a big brother now!"
Dad showed Luke a photo on his mobile phone.
A shriveled red monkey was looking at Luke from the phone screen. Luke was confused. The monkey was not at all like those beautiful little children from the books that Mom showed to him.
"Who is this?" Luke asked.
"What do you mean?" Dad looked puzzled. "It's your little sister. She was born today."
Luke frowned.
He knew that Mom was going to have a baby, but he never expected to see this red, screaming girl with small eyes and very little hair.

Luke wanted to ask Dad about that, but Dad was gone.
He raced around the kitchen on the phone to all his friends, telling them about his new daughter.

"She's 21 inches and 7 pounds!" Dad exclaimed proudly.

And Luke?
Luke went to his room and went to bed. It was quite late and time to sleep. Luke was waiting for his dad to come to read him a book, but Dad did not come. Luke could only hear Dad talking loudly and very happily on the phone.

Luke felt sad. How could Dad forget to come to him? Is this red monkey more important now? Feeling a bit sad, Luke fell asleep.

Two days passed.
"Luke, get ready!" Dad commanded. "We're going to bring Mom and your little sister home."
Luke got ready very quickly. He put on a new T-shirt and even combed his hair. He was interested to see his sister. He was still hoping that she now looked like the child from the picture book. But most of all, Luke wanted to see his mom. He missed Mom very much.

When Luke and his dad arrived at the hospital, they had to wait a little.
And then Mom came out. She was carrying a small bundle of blankets in her hands. Mom immediately went up to Luke, hugged him, and kissed him.
"Oh, Luke! You've turned into such a big boy!" Mom said with tears in her eyes.
"In three days?" Luke asked.
"In three days," Mom sighed. "Look who we have."

Mom brought the bundle to Luke and opened it slightly. Luke saw the same face as on the phone, only not as red as before. It was so small. The girl's eyes were closed—she was fast asleep.
"Would you like to hold her?" Mom asked. "Put out your hands!"
Mom put his sister in Luke's arms but still kept hold of the little girl.
"Careful, don't drop her!" Mom said.

"We will bathe her together this evening!" Dad said. He took the baby from Luke and went to the car. Luke and his mom followed.

At home, Luke's sister was now the center of attention. As soon as she woke up, she started crying. Mom and Dad were both running around her, and they weren't interested in anything else. Luke didn't like it one bit.

Luke sat out of the way, but he expected to be noticed. He was hungry—it was long past lunchtime. Only no one noticed it. So Luke took a piece of bread from the kitchen and went to his room. Why sit with your parents if they don't care?

On the way, Luke looked in the mirror.
"How can Mom and Dad love this little screaming girl so much? I'm much more handsome. And I've more hair. And I don't scream all the time. Could it be that since I grew up, they are no longer interested in me?" Luke thought.

Luke sat in his room and cried. Suddenly, the door opened, and Mom walked in.

Luke really wanted to run to his mom and hug her, but he was too upset with her! It was a strange feeling. He turned away from her.

"You don't have to be here if you would prefer to be with her," he said crossly.

"Oh darling." Mom sat down on the floor next to Luke and hugged him tightly. "There is no need to be jealous. I am sorry I haven't been paying any attention to you. I'm just not used to having a baby again. Don't be jealous. I love you very much!"

"As much as you love her?" Luke asked.

"I love you like the best boy in the whole world—my son, and I'm so proud of you!"

"And do you love her as much?"

"Yes, I love you both the same!" Mom answered.

"But you used to love me more than anyone else! I was always in the first place!"

"I understand that you want me to be always only with you and you alone," Mom said. "But your little sister Emma can't live without me now. She can't even hold her head up."

"What do you mean, she can't hold her head up? Will it fall off?" Luke did not understand.

"Come, and I'll show you." Mom smiled. She took Luke by the hand and led him down.

Dad was sitting downstairs on the couch. And in front of him, on a blanket, lay Emma. She was not wrapped up, so Luke could carefully examine her. He looked closer and saw that she had long eyelashes, the same as Dad's. And her hands were tiny.

Luke wanted to touch her hand with his finger, and Emma grabbed it tightly. She stared at Luke and ... smiled!
"Look, she is smiling!" Mom laughed. "Luke, she is smiling at you! You see how much she loves you!"
Luke was so happy. She smiled at him! Not at Mom, not at Dad, but at him! Luke loved his new sister!

That day Luke learned that being jealous is a very unpleasant feeling. Mom and Dad have so much love that they have enough for both him and his little sister. And in his heart, too, there is enough love for everyone!

Despair and Compassion

Uncle Sam came to visit! Brilliant! Uncle Sam traveled a lot and always had interesting stories to tell. He always came with a gift for Luke. I wonder, what he brought this time?
Wow! Uncle Sam brought a kite. Not the usual kite, but the best one Luke had ever seen! It was shaped liked a dragon—red with golden scales. It had a long tail that fluttered in the wind. Luke had been dreaming of having a cool kite for such a long time! It was perfect!

"Let's go fly the kite!" Luke asked Uncle Sam.
"We'll go soon, but first, let me talk to your dad a little bit and eat something," promised Uncle Sam. "It's windy today. Perfect kite-flying weather."
Luke couldn't wait. What if the wind died down?
"I'll go with Lilly. We'll be at the soccer field!" Luke shouted, running out of the house.

The weather was indeed perfect. The wind was blowing not too strong but enough for the kite to fly. Luke knew how to fly a kite. He had already done it with Dad, even though that time the kite had got tangled up in a tree. Here, on the soccer field, there were no trees, so nothing could go wrong.

"Wow!" Lilly exclaimed when Luke launched the kite for the first time. A real huge dragon was flying in the sky near the school! Luke and Lilly stood amazed.

"Can I try?" Lilly asked.
"Okay, just hold on tight," Luke warned. "You should never let go, or it will fly away."
"I'll hold tight. I promise!" Lilly agreed. So Luke let the kite fall back to earth and handed the rope to Lilly.

Lilly couldn't get the kite to fly right away. But Luke helped her. Finally, Lilly's dragon was flying in the sky.
"Hurrah! It flies!" Lilly shouted happily.
"Now it's my turn," Luke commanded. "Please pass me the rope!"
So Lilly passed the rope to Luke.
"Look how high it can fly!"

Luke began to unwind the rope. The kite flew higher and higher! It was high in the sky! A real dragon! But suddenly ...

A strong wind blew and pulled the rope from Luke's hands. Luke hadn't expected that. He dropped the rope. The dragon spread its wings wide and flew up and away into the sky.
Luke and Lilly jumped, trying to grab on to the rope, but the kite flew further and further away from them.

Luke was in despair.
"I can't believe it!" he screamed. "A-A-A-A-A-A-A-A."
Luke's scream was not like his usual voice.
He felt pain in his chest. His legs became weak and stopped holding him up. He fell to the ground, curled up into a ball, and covered his head with his hands.
"It's lost," Luke kept repeating.

For Luke, it was the end of the world.
Lilly sank to the ground and sat down next to Luke. She stroked him, and tears streamed down her cheeks. She felt so sorry for Luke. He looked so sad. Lilly felt his pain and really wanted to help him.

"Don't cry, Luke," Lilly said. "We will buy a new kite!"
"We'll never find such a cool one! Uncle Sam bought it for me from another country! It's gone!" Luke continued to sob.
"We'll fix that!" Lilly insisted. "I have coins and even one banknote in my piggy bank. I'll give them to you. All of them! I do not mind! And you have coins. Let's go count and ask Uncle Sam to buy you a new kite, an even better one!"

Luke and Lilly went to Lilly's house and counted Lilly's coins. And then Luke's coins. Mom and Dad also gave some money. Uncle Sam promised to buy a new kite—an even better one.
So, everything was fine again!

Luke Beats His Anger

Luke knocked on Lilly's door and shouted, "Lilly, come! Let's play in our garden. My dad will soon be grilling sausages."
"I can't," Lilly answered. "I'm going to a birthday party. Remember, I told you?"
Lilly was dressed smartly and was holding a present in her hands. She was about to leave.
"What gift do you have?" Luke asked.
"A treasure hunt card game about pirates and a real pirate hat. Cool, huh?" Lilly showed Luke the hat.

Luke was upset. Of course—Lilly was going to the new trampoline park for a birthday party! She had also bought the cool card game that they saw together in the store. It wasn't fair!

Luke went home and climbed into his treehouse. He had an unpleasant feeling. Why didn't Lilly ask if he could come with her? He didn't have a lot of friends here. And this card game ...

So, Luke decided that he would draw the card game for himself. Just where did his colored pencils go? He brought them here ... Luke looked around for his pencils. Here they were!
Luke reached for the pencil jar, and ... it fell out of his hands. The pencils scattered all across the floor and broke.
"Stupid pencils. Where is the sharpener?" Luke thought.
But he couldn't find it.
So, Luke had to go home to search.

"Ouch," Luke shouted as he tumbled down the stairs. He was in such a hurry to go down that he missed a step and was now lying on the ground, rubbing his bottom. "Stupid stairs."
Luke got up and kicked the ladder with all his might, but that only hurt even more.
"Hrhrhrhrhr," Luke growled.
He felt very hot as if a fire was burning in his cheeks. His heart pounded strongly. He clenched his fists and walked swiftly toward the house.

At the house, he was met by his grandfather.
"Hi, Luke!" Grandpa said happily. "Let's make paper airplanes and launch them."
"No, I am not interested!" Luke shouted angrily. He pushed past his grandfather, went into his room, and slammed the door loudly behind him.

Luke sat in the room and breathed loudly. He was angry with the whole world! Soon there was a knock on his door. The door opened, and his grandfather carefully stepped in.
"Do you want to talk?" he asked quietly.
Luke didn't answer.
Grandpa sank to the floor next to Luke.
"What made you so angry?" he asked.
"How do you know?" Luke was surprised.

Grandpa grinned.
"Well, it's not hard to see. When a person is very angry, others can always see it. Now many things can make you angry. For example, I am always a little angry when I am hungry. And some people get angry when they envy someone or when they get nervous before some important event. Do you know what an iceberg looks like?"
Grandpa reached over to the table, took a piece of paper and a pencil, and began to draw.

"An iceberg," continued Grandpa, "is a huge piece of ice. But you can't see it fully. It is almost entirely hidden underwater. What you can see is only a small piece at the top. So, anger is like that visible piece but below the surface are all sorts of feelings that have caused it. So, what has made you so angry?"

Luke told his grandfather what had happened.
"Ah, I see," Grandpa said. "You could not stop your anger in time, and it grew and grew until it exploded. It's like a thermometer. When you become ill, your temperature rises. If you take medicine on time, the temperature will drop, and you will feel good again. But if you do nothing, it will grow and grow, and you will feel worse and worse. Therefore, my little man, you need to learn to stop your anger in time."
"Easier said than done," Luke said thoughtfully.
"Oh, it's not that difficult. The main thing is to know how. In fact, you already know a lot yourself.

"The best thing is to walk away. It is easier to calm down when you are away from the thing that annoys you.

"Take ten deep breaths—slowly breathe in through your nose and breathe out through your mouth while counting one, two, three, four, five, six, seven, eight, nine, ten.

"Squeeze the anger in your hands and then let it go. You can also draw your anger on a piece of paper, scrunch it up and throw it away.

"You can even do an angry dance. Or punch an angry cushion. When there is too much anger in you, moving helps you get rid of it."

"What a bad feeling!" Luke exhaled. "It would be better if it didn't exist."
"Not at all," Grandpa said. "Anger can be a very useful feeling. Perhaps people would not have survived in ancient times without it."

Luke looked at his grandfather in surprise.
"Guess which feeling helped people long ago hunt animals? It was anger. Which feeling helps animals protect their children when they are in danger? Also anger. What helps athletes win competitions? Yes, it's often anger. Anger gives a person courage and determination, so it is essential. Remember: even if we sometimes get angry in our family, we still love each other very much. Anger is like the wind: it blows, and then it stops. And love doesn't go anywhere."

Luke smiled, hugged Grandpa tightly, and said, "Sorry, Grandpa. My anger is all gone. Let's go make paper planes together?"

Feeling Shy and Self-conscious

Do you know what Murphy's Law is?
According to this law, everything that can go wrong, will go wrong.

Lilly was celebrating her birthday! What a wonderful day!
Lilly's entire house was decorated with beautiful ribbons and balloons! Even the gate of the house was decorated with balloons. And the number 7 was glued to the front door so that everyone would know what a special day it was!

And what about Luke? Luke was ready.
Mom helped him buy a gift—a globe! And a big beautiful balloon! And a bar of chocolate! So many gifts!

When suddenly ... Luke's tooth fell out. His very front tooth! All would be fine, but one couldn't just see it. One could hear it too. When Luke wanted to say "soup", he said "thoop." Instead of "soap" he said "thoap." And instead of "sing" he said "thing." Mom and Dad found it to be sweet and funny, but Luke didn't.

"I'm not going to Lilly's birthday!" Luke said stubbornly.
"But why?" Mom couldn't understand. "How can you not go to a friend's birthday?"
"Tell them that I'm thick," Luke asked Mom. He wanted to say "sick," but it came out as "thick."
"I won't," Mom replied. "I don't want to lie! What are you thinking of?"
"I don't want everyone to laugh at me when I thpeak," Luke said sadly.
"Okay, then don't go." Mom seemed to agree. "I saw Lilly's mom buying prizes for the riddle quiz," she said slyly. "Let other kids win them."

So Luke, of course, went to Lilly's birthday party.

There were many children in Lilly's house, many of whom Luke saw for the first time.
"This is my cousin Tanya." Lilly introduced her to Luke. "And this is my friend Tom."
Luke couldn't memorize all the names. He tried not to open his mouth and not to speak. Luke was very shy. He was afraid that if he opened his mouth, everyone would laugh at him.

Everything went to plan. He had managed to sit on the edge of the party for most of it. But he was very bored. He so wanted to play games, scream, and shout, but he stayed away with his

mouth closed. An inner voice told him, "Go play. No one will laugh. Everything will be fine!" But Luke continued to be shy. How can you not be self-conscious when there are so many strangers around, and you cannot speak normally ...

And then Lilly's mom took out a bag with prizes.
"Attention everyone who wants to win a prize! We are starting our riddle quiz. For every correct answer—a prize!

"Question number 1:
I am an animal which is known as the king of the jungle. Who am I?"
Well, that was a straightforward question! Luke knew the answer. It was a lion!
Luke did not know what to do—he knew the correct answer but hesitated to say. And while Luke thought about what to do, Tom gave the correct answer and got a stuffed lion toy!

Lilly's mom continued.
"Question number 2:
I am a long animal that can eat leaves from very high trees. My legs are long and strong enough to kill the king of the jungle. Who am I?"
Luke's mind was thinking quickly. Long neck ... Long legs ...
"It's a giraffe!" shouted a girl with pigtails, and she got a small giraffe.

"Question number 3:
I am small and shy. I have eight legs. I catch insects and eat them. Who am I?"
Luke couldn't stand it! Everyone was silent, and he knew the answer! Luke's hands were sweating. His heart was pounding. Luke gathered all his courage and shouted out loudly, **"Thpider! Fpider!"** he repeated.

It was terrible! Luke couldn't pronounce the word correctly!

He felt himself getting smaller and closed his eyes, expecting everyone to laugh.

"Exactly! **Thpider! Hpider! Fpider!**" he heard from all sides. And everyone laughed. And Lilly's mother laughed. And Luke also laughed. And everyone had a lot of fun!

"It's great when you can be yourself!" Luke said to his mom and dad when they came to kiss him before going to bed. "And there was no need to be shy at all. We are all different, and that's what makes life interesting!"

And Luke cuddled the prize he had won—a little hairy spider.

Mom and Dad kissed Luke and left. And he still could not sleep. He lay and thought.

Life was full of surprises. When he recently left his friends, he was sorrowful. It seemed that his whole world had turned upside down. But that was not the case at all.

Now he has Lilly—a funny girl who is such a good friend.
He has a little sister who loves him.
He has grandparents nearby who give him so much attention.
He has a mom and dad, for whom he is the best boy in the world.
And yes, he also has those old friends who are far away but still with him.

After moving to a new house, Luke got into many different situations and experienced new and different feelings. Some were pleasant. Some were not. But they were all natural and helped him. And they made his life so bright.

However, he always had one more feeling in all these situations, the most important and most pleasant feeling.
He was loved!
At this thought, Luke smiled and drifted off to sleep.

I hope this book helped your children understand that all our feelings are very normal and can be used by us in many positive ways.

If that is the case, please spread the word.
By leaving a review you will help other parents raise happy and self-confident kids!

How does SAD feel in my body?

I don't want to eat.

I want to go home.

My eyes feel watery, and I want to cry.

My whole body feels down.

I want to snuggle in a safe place.

Nothing excites me.

What helps me when I feel SAD?

☐ talk to someone

ask for a hug ☐

☐ do something I enjoy

think of a happy memory ☐

☐ get a drink of water

write a letter ☐

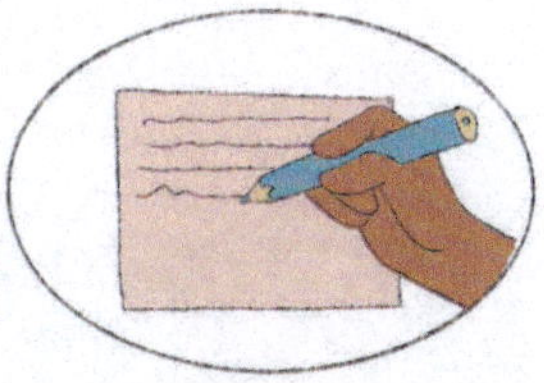

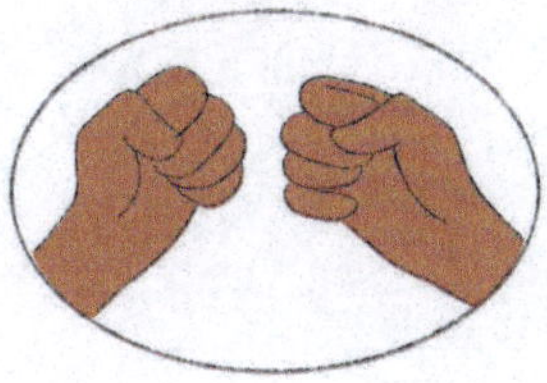

☐ squeeze then relax my muscles

take extra long breaths ☐

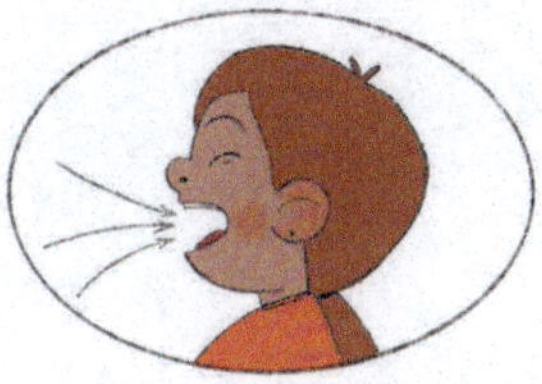

☐ read a book

tell to myself — all will be good ☐

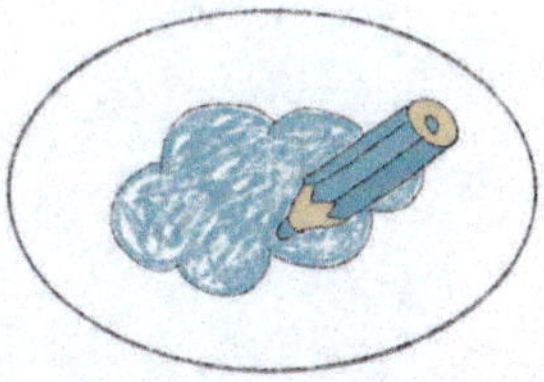

☐ draw or color

stretch ☐

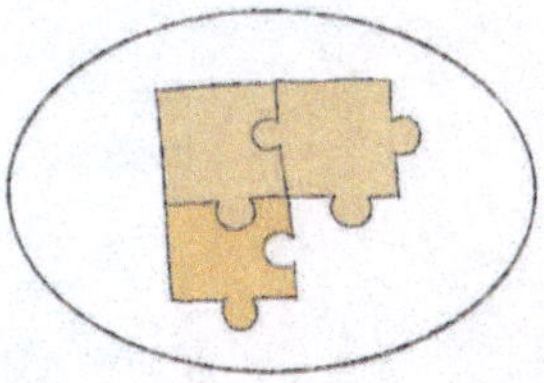

☐ build something or do a puzzle

give my stuffed animal a hug ☐

What inspires ME?

Please think of examples.

Books

Music

Nature

Art

Pictures

People

Events

Food

Color

Sport

This is someone whom I miss and want to see again soon

I can breathe like that

Lazy 8 Breathing

Draw a number 8 while slowly breathing in through your nose and breathing out through your mouth.

Bubble Breathing

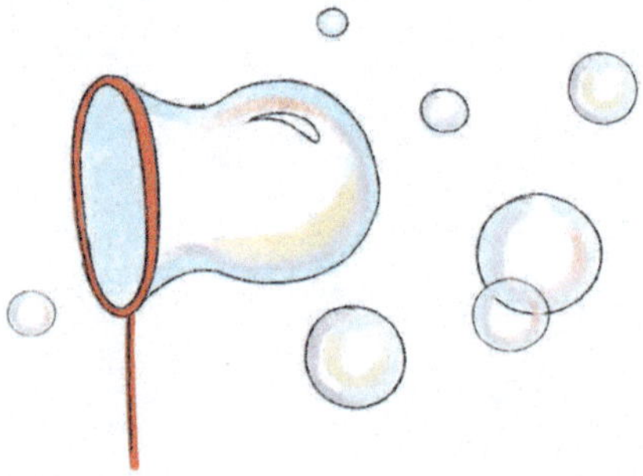

Imagine, that you are blowing bubbles. Take a deep breath through your nose and slowly breathe out through your mouth.

Rainbow Breathing

Travel the rainbow from one cloud to the other. Breathe in when you travel to the right and out when you travel back. Trace every color.

Balloon Belly

Imagine a balloon in your tummy. Can you blow it big by taking a deep breath? Then, breathe out. Try again!

This is what I am proud of

I can think positively

I went fishing but did not catch anything.

I almost won a running competition but at the very last moment I lost.

My little brother broke the LEGO castle that was nearly done. Now I have to start again.

My friend Fin got sick and our sleepover got cancelled at the last minute.

I thought Anna was my friend, but today I heard her saying bad things about me behind my back.

I've studied so much for this test. I was sure I would do well. However, I did not. Why am I such a looser?

I like building LEGO castles. I can build an even better one next time. Shall I ask my friend Tom to come and build it with me?

I've learned my lesson. I should have spent more time preparing for the test. Good that I still have enough time to prepare well for the next one.

The weather was great. It was so enjoyable to be out!

It's good that now I know I should be careful with her. I was lucky to learn that before I told her all my secrets.

I did well! It was a great way to prepare myself for future competitions. And it was so much fun!

It's not so bad. Al least now I have enough time to finish this interesting book I am reading. I can have a sleepover at Fin's house once he feels better.

Cross out what is wrong

Understand what you've done wrong.

Come up with a plan to fix things.

When I feel ASHAMED I can...

Apologize.

Try to forget about it.

Blame someone else for it.

Never admit your guilt.

Ask an adult for an advice.

I can draw MY FEAR ...

... in a FUN way

Cross out what is wrong

Say "It is not fair! Friends do not do such things!"

Don't say anything, just walk away.

When I am OFFENDED I can...

Don't tell anyone.

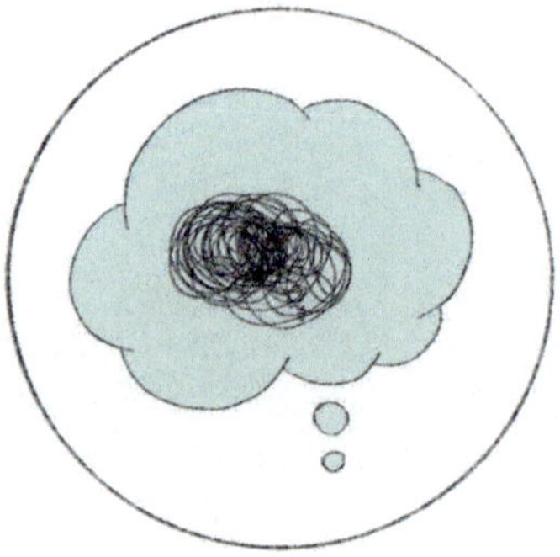

Just try to forget about it.

Explain, what exactly offended you.

Suggest a plan to fix things.

Ask an adult for an advice.

How I can use my Worry Dolls

I put them under my pillow at night, to take my worries away.

I tell my worries to them.

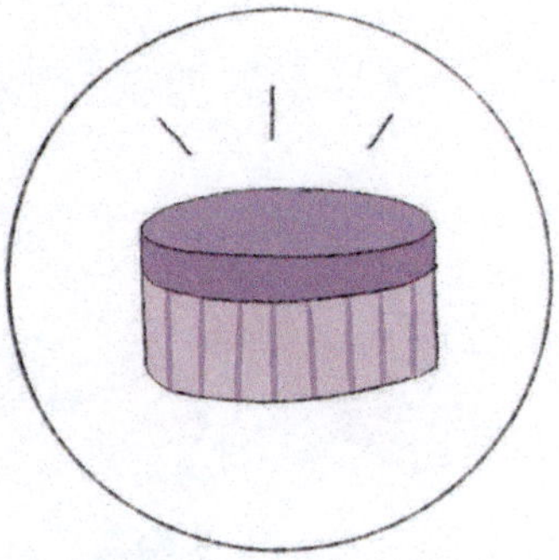

I keep them in a box and take them out only when I need their help.

I sail them away to take my worries away.

I give them cute and funny names.

My steps to solve a problem

These phrases help me on the way

Cross out what is wrong

I say "Stop! You have no right to do that!"

I pretend that nothing is wrong.

I agree to do as they say.

I ask my friends to help me.

How I stand up to bullies...

I stand up straight. Hold my head up.

I try to hide so that bullies do not see me.

I don't tell an adult.

I tell an adult.

I don't show that I am upset.

What
makes me
special?

Self-esteem sunglasses

I can use self-esteem glasses

My positive thoughts and affirmations

1. I have many talents.
2. I have a great personality.
3. I am a good person.
4. Today is going to be a great day for me.
5. Making mistakes helps me grow.
6. My thoughts and feelings are important.
7. It's my character, not my appearance, that counts.
8. I love being me.
9. I am perfect the way I am.
10. I am special and unique.
11. I have a big heart.
12. I love my body.
13. I don't have to be perfect to be worthy.
14. I don't have to follow the crowd.
15. Today I choose to be proud of myself.
16. It's ok to take time for yourself.
17. My family loves me for the person I am.
18. If I want to, there is nothing in this world I cannot do.
19. I am kind and friendly; that's why people around me enjoy my company.
20. I remember that bad feelings come and go.
21. Every day brings a new opportunity.
22. I'm not afraid of a challenge.
23. Next time I will do my best.
24. Challenges make me strong.
25. I get back up when I fall.
26. I am capable of more than I know
27. I am proud to be different.
28. Today is a fresh start.
29. Giving my best is enough.
30. I can choose to think positively when things are hard
31. I am building my future.
32. I can learn anything I put my mind to.
33. All of my problems have solutions.
34. I can cheer myself up when I'm down.
35. I will have a great day no matter what.
36. My thoughts and feelings are important.
37. I can stand up for what I believe in.
38. It's OK to ask for help.
39. I'm fun to be around.
40. I am not afraid of problems, and I am smart enough to solve them.
41. No matter if people say I cannot do it, I know I can.
42. If I don't get it right the first time, I can try again
43. I get better every single day.
44. I feel happy and excited to experience new things.
45. Today, I will shine.
46. I am a natural winner.
47. I choose joy.
48. I can be anything I want to be.
49. I deserve to be loved.
50. I am open and ready to learn.

I can say "I am sorry"

When I am in despair...

I can scream it out.

It's ok to cry.

I know my grief will go away, even though it is hard to believe.

It helps to talk to my parents about it.

I can make a memory box.

I can ask for a hug.

A worry doll can help too.

How can I help to someone in despair?

My Anger Warning Signs

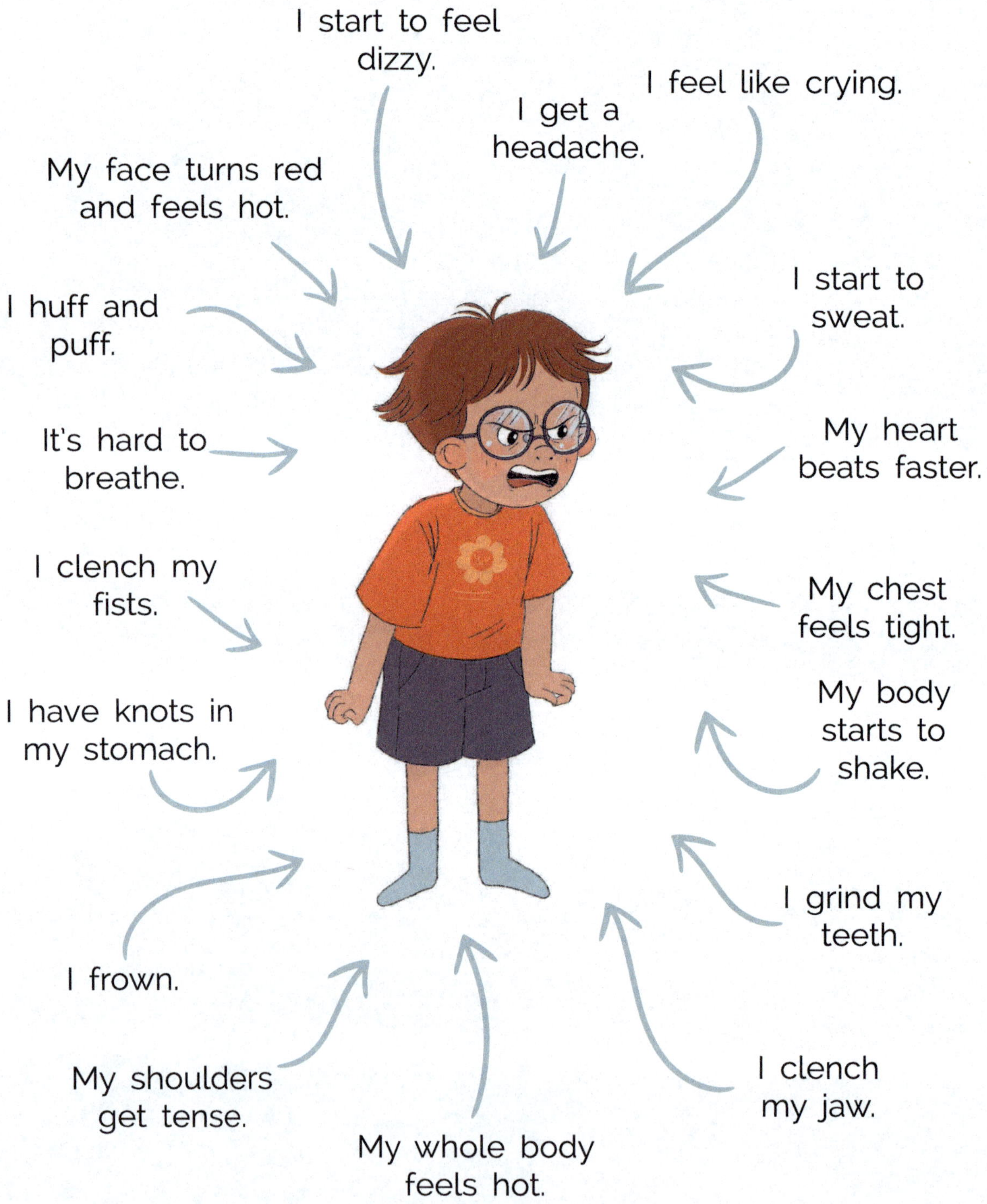

What can make me angry

My anger thermometer

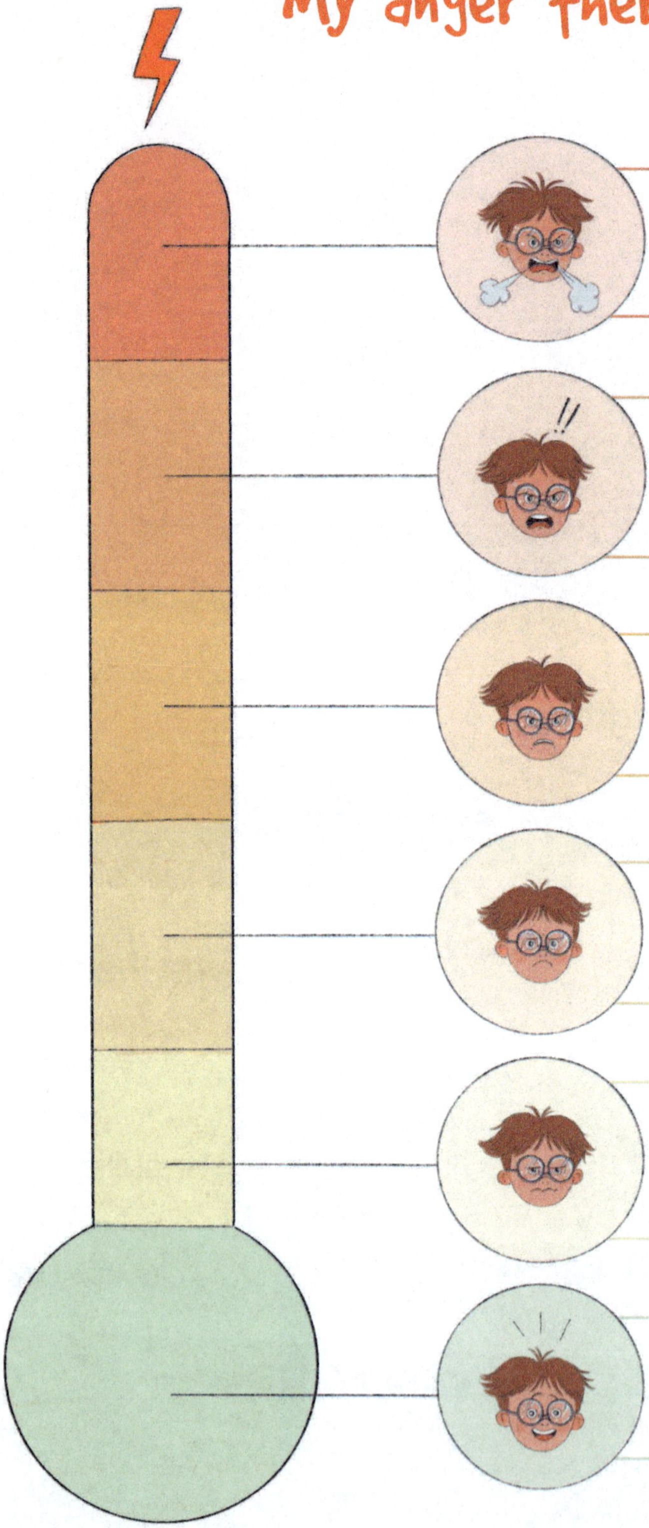

I can't stay in control of my anger and can hurt myself or others.

I feel very uncomfortable and find it hard to think clearly.

I feel uncomfortable and start trembling inside.

I am really not happy about what is happening.

Something is bothering me and I can get angry if that does not stop

I feel calm and relaxed. All is good.

Helpful or not?

Cross out what is wrong

This helps me calm down when I am angry

Count to 20.

Bounce a ball.

Stretch or do yoga.

Anger rescue kit.

Drink some water.

Breathing exercises.

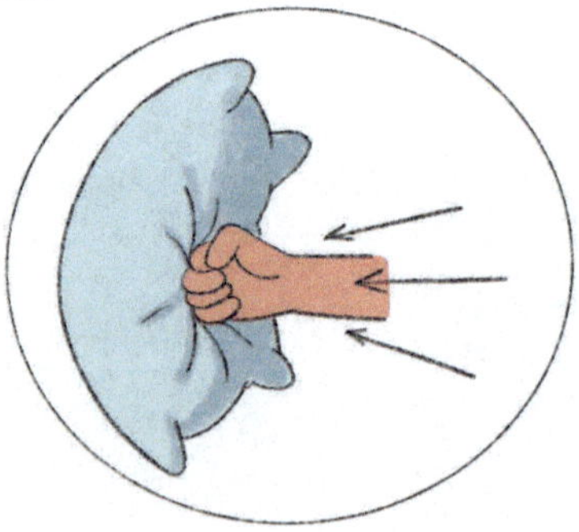

Punch a pillow.

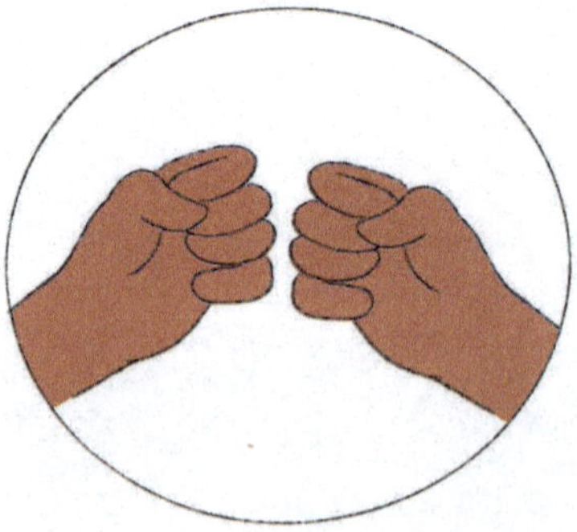

Squeeze and then release my muscles.

Use my deep breathing techniques.

Write about your anger.

Draw your anger.

Do 50 Jumping Jacks.

Push a wall.

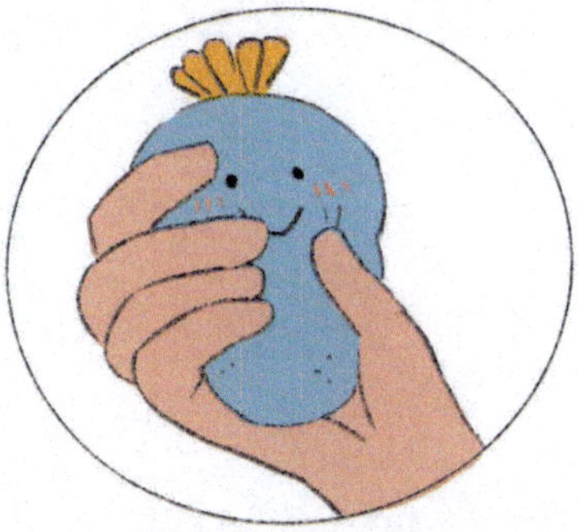

Take it out on a squishy.

Talk about your anger.

Take a break.

What I love about my sibling(s)

All worksheets from this book can be downloaded as .pdf files from the website

www.maguirebooks.com

Notes:

Printed in Great Britain
by Amazon

21439226R00088